DARWINISM

TODAY

DIVIDED LABOURS

··

AN EVOLUTIONARY VIEW OF
WOMEN AT WORK

Kingsley Browne

Weidenfeld & Nicolson
LONDON

First published in Great Britain in 1998 by
Weidenfeld & Nicolson
The Orion Publishing Group Ltd
Orion House
5 Upper Saint Martin's Lane
London, WC2H 9EA

Foreword © 1998 Helena Cronin and Oliver Curry

A CIP catalogue record for this book is available
from the British Library.

ISBN 0 297 84140 8

Typeset by SetSystems Ltd, Saffron Walden, Essex

Set in 11/13 Bembo

Printed in Great Britain by Clays Ltd, St Ives plc

CONTENTS

The Series Editors thank
Geoffrey Miller and
Peter Tallack for their help

FOREWORD

Darwinism Today is a series of short books by leading figures in the field of evolutionary theory. Each title is an authoritative pocket introduction to the Darwinian ideas that are setting today's intellectual agenda.

The series developed out of the Darwin@LSE programme at the London School of Economics. The Darwin Seminars provide a platform for distinguished evolutionists to present the latest Darwinian thinking and to explore its application to humans. The programme is having an enormous impact, both in helping to popularize evolutionary theory and in fostering cross-disciplinary approaches to shared problems.

With the publication of **Darwinism Today** we hope that the best of the new Darwinian ideas will reach an even wider audience.

Helena Cronin and Oliver Curry
Series Editors

DIVIDED LABOURS

....

**AN EVOLUTIONARY VIEW OF
WOMEN AT WORK**

INTRODUCTION

Human beings are animals and so have been shaped by the same forces of natural selection as have constructed all other animals. Most people have no trouble accepting that our upright locomotion, large brains, and opposable thumbs are products of natural selection, as are behavioural differences between, say, lions and chimpanzees. More controversial, however, is the suggestion that the same forces as produced human bodies and 'chimpanzee nature' also produced a 'human nature'. Yet the mechanisms that shape human behaviour, no less than those that shape human anatomy and physiology, are products of the fundamental laws of biology.

Over the last three decades, theoretical and empirical work in biology, psychology, and anthropology has undercut the reigning view that human behaviour is largely independent of biology, as well as the concomitant view that animal behaviour is largely fixed by biology. It turns out that animal behaviour is more environmentally sensitive and human behaviour more biologically influenced than previously believed.

One of the leading insights of the recent scholarship is confirmation of the popular view that there are substantial psychological differences between men and women.

But the public-policy literature, whilst conceding a difference in reproductive biology, largely ignores sex differences that extend to temperament and behaviour. The prevailing view in the social sciences is that any behavioural sex differences that exist are products of differences in child-rearing practices and cultural influences. Yet the anthropological literature alone demonstrates a remarkable cross-cultural consistency in the sex differences under consideration, and the biological and psychological literatures are bulging with data revealing robust differences between the sexes. This literature suggests that we may have been confusing cause and effect; our patriarchal social structure – to the extent we have one – may be more an effect of sex differences than their cause.

The burden of biology

It is a testament to the strength of our desire to disbelieve the existence of biological sex differences that those asserting such differences bear an often insurmountable burden of proof. Readers should consider discussions about sex differences to which they have been privy; an assertion that the difference at issue is caused by socialization typically goes unchallenged, while assertion of a biological cause usually evokes an expression of scepticism and a demand for proof.

Some believe that the existence of social reinforcements makes a biological cause unlikely. But the existence of social inputs does not imply the lack of a biological contribution. Indeed, their existence implies a psychological architecture specifically designed to pick up on these salient pieces of information. The fact that parents pressure children to eat their dinners does not imply that children's hunger is 'socially constructed'.

Biologically influenced sex differences in behaviour are not inherently improbable; indeed, if they do not exist in humans, humans are unique among sexually reproducing species. These sex differences could have important ramifications in the workplace, yet the current debate over the roles of the sexes at work generally rests on the assumption that the sexes are temperamentally identical.

Consider discussions about the 'glass ceiling'. The 'glass ceiling' is a metaphor that describes the under-representation of women in the upper reaches of management. Although women constitute approximately 40 per cent of the US workforce – and, indeed, 40 per cent of all managers – they hold only 5 to 7 per cent of senior executive positions. The term 'glass ceiling' is a clever metaphor for it not only captures an empirical observation – that women's progression up the corporate hierarchy tends to 'stall' at some point – but it also contains within it an assumption that the causes are unrelated to inherent sex differences and entirely the result of invisible forces internal to the organization but external to women.

Discussion of the 'gender gap' in earnings also assumes identity of the sexes. The term 'gender gap' describes the difference between average earnings of full-time male and female employees, typically expressed as the ratio of women's earnings to men's. In the United States, women earn about seventy-five cents for every dollar earned by men, although for younger women the gap is much smaller. Like the term 'glass ceiling', the term 'gender gap' is loaded in that it implies that the cause is employer oppression of women that necessarily requires correction, rather than recognizing that the gap may reflect evolved differences between the sexes, which would require the merits of 'correction' to be debated rather than assumed.

The 1995 report of the United States Glass Ceiling Commission, entitled *Good For Business: Making Full Use of the Nation's Human Capital,* sought an explanation in societal and corporate barriers. If one lacked preconceived notions about the cause, however, one might cast a broader net. Although there might indeed be attributes of the corporation or society that impede achievement by women, there might also be something intrinsic to men and women themselves – differences in interest, ability, temperament, or qualifications – that leads to differential outcomes.

Suppose, for example, that men are more competitive than women by nature and more inclined to expend effort to climb corporate hierarchies. Would it be unfair if a disproportionate number of men achieved the highest positions in the hierarchy? Suppose also that men are more inclined to take 'career risks' than women. If men are more willing to put themselves into positions where there is substantial possibility of failure, would it be unfair if more of the great successes – and great failures – turn out to be men? Suppose that men place a higher priority than women on acquiring resources; would it be unfair if those most willing to sacrifice other areas of their lives acquire more resources than those for whom resource acquisition is less of a priority?

4

Conversely, suppose that women are inclined to be more attached to their children and less willing to sacrifice time spent with them for material resources. If the satisfaction women receive from devotion to family outweighs the economic satisfaction they gain from the workplace, should we denounce the choices they make?

It might sound terribly sexist to suggest that men are more competitive, more driven towards acquisition of status and resources, and more inclined to take risks; and that women are more nurturing, risk averse, less greedy, and less single-minded. So let me make clear what is being argued. It is the central thesis of this book that much of the glass ceiling and gender gap is the product of basic biological sex differences in personality and temperament acting in the context of the modern labour market. These differences have resulted from differential reproductive strategies followed by the two sexes during the course of human evolution and are as much a product of natural selection as our bipedal locomotion and opposable thumbs.

It is not here suggested, however, that biology is the exclusive cause of the glass ceiling or the gender gap; social attitudes, some of them arbitrary, as well as outright sex discrimination based upon false assumptions about the relative capacities of the sexes, also play a role. Moreover, no argument is made here that the labour market cannot be changed in ways that would at least reduce the economic disparity between men and women. Most obviously, of course, the state could intervene to redistribute the prizes of competition or prevent competition from yielding such prizes in the first place. The wage gap is considerably smaller in

Australia than in the United States, for example, as a consequence of Australia's centralization of wage determination, higher rates of unionization, lower wage inequality generally, and adoption of comparable-worth policies. Whether such a course should be followed in other countries is a policy question rather than a scientific one. However, policy makers should take humans as they are − rather than as they would like them to be − when crafting their policies.

The task of social policy

Some people may resist reliance upon one view or another of human nature as a basis for formulating policy. Many fear that appeals to a biological human nature are a subterfuge to maintain the status quo. But this needn't be the case. Indeed, what could be more essential to world harmony than the recognition that we are all basically the same once the superficial differences of our cultures are stripped away? A belief in human nature is essential to a belief in the psychic unity of mankind and ultimately to a belief in human rights and democracy. Recognition of a fundamental human nature acknowledges that human behaviour is not infinitely malleable, but it does not deny the autonomy and dignity of the individual.

When one thinks about it, almost all discussions of public policy rest on an implicit view of human nature. Government programmes that are structured to create incentives, for example, are based on a belief that the incentive will modify behaviour. Put another way, they are based on a belief that a particular environmental modification acting on a human organism will result in predictable behavioural change. Such a prediction is impossible without at least an implicit theory of the mind. Similarly, much policy relating to sexual equality is based upon the standard social-science assumption that there is one human nature shared by both sexes, rather than, as argued here, a male nature and a female nature. Thus, it is not a question of whether one should have a view of human nature, but rather a question of which view of human nature one should have.

....

CHAPTER 1

Sex Differences and Evolutionary Theory

Natural selection

Living organisms possess heritable features built by their genes. Those genes that build features that help the organism to survive and reproduce will, down the generations, become more prevalent than those that do not. The process of change in gene frequencies and in the features that genes build is called evolution by natural selection.

Charles Darwin (1809–82) tended to concentrate on traits such as shape, size and colour, but the propagation of the organism's genes is also dependent upon the organism's behaviour. Birds migrate, salmon swim upstream to spawn, and mammalian mothers nurture their young. Like the various features of the animal's anatomy, the psychological mechanisms that produce behaviour are subject to the forces of natural selection.

Sexual selection

Many of the traits Darwin studied had obvious functional significance and were clearly related to survival. He described numerous animals whose traits protected them against the hostile forces of nature: temperature, moisture, drought, hunger, predators, and so forth. Because those forces present dangers to both sexes, there are few sex differences in the evolved mechanisms that deal with them.

Darwin further observed, however, that many traits could not be explained as adaptations to these natural forces. A classic example is the peacock's tail. The peacock's long, brightly plumed tail would appear to imperil its survival by making it more visible to predators and interfering with mobility. Darwin correctly concluded that the peacock's tail was functional because it helped the peacock attract a mate, a form of selection he termed 'sexual selection'. Because each sex presents its own adaptive challenges to the other, there are differences in the respective evolved mechanisms designed to deal with them. So, male ornamentation evolved, according to Darwin, because peahens are attracted to it and preferentially mate with the most ornamental males. Thus, peahens evolved the sophisticated perceptual system necessary to discriminate among the various strutting suitors.

Besides evolution driven by female choice, Darwin described another form of sexual selection: male–male competition. A classic example is the antlers of a male deer. Male deer seldom use their antlers against predators, but rather against other male deer – their competitors for females. During the rutting season, males engage in combat and to the victors belong the spoils – access to females. Despite the apparent disadvantage of carrying about a weapon that is physiologically expensive to create and maintain, a large rack of antlers gives its owner an advantage in the centrally important mating game. Whether a specific form of sexual selection is characterized as 'female choice' or 'male-male competition', it involves greater competition between males than between females – in our examples, either in growing the desired plumage or in growing and using deadly weapons.

Reproductive strategies

That men and women should have different reproductive strategies is not intuitively obvious. After all, they are members of the same species, and the reproductive success of men is critically dependent upon women, and vice versa. Therefore, the interests of men and women might seem totally congruent.

However, the battle of the sexes goes back almost to the origins of sexual reproduction itself. It has been demonstrated that a situation in which each sex contributes gametes (sex cells) of equal size to produce offspring is not stable. Over evolutionary time, organisms contributing equal-sized gametes will always be ousted by those contributing gametes of unequal sizes, the larger gamete carrying greater nutrients and the smaller being more numerous and more mobile. Once this process is started, it tends to be self-reinforcing, those that give more, specializing in giving yet more, and those that give less giving even less.

From this arbitrary specialization flows the sexual division of reproductive labour. When zoologists define the sexes according to the size of their sex cell – the sex with the smaller cell is male – they are acknowledging the fundamental process that is responsible for the divergent reproductive strategies we see in all sexual species.

Nowhere is this more obvious than in mammalian reproduction. Although the act of intercourse in humans requires only a few minutes of time for both sexes, if it leads to conception, the consequent burdens on the two partners are grossly asymmetrical. The woman must carry and nourish the baby for nine months, and, thereafter, in a traditional society at any rate, she must nurse it. Even after weaning, the child requires care by adults (although by this time the burden can be shared).

In 1972, biologist Robert Trivers coined the term 'parental investment' to refer to 'any investment by the parent in an individual offspring that increases the off-spring's chance of surviving (and hence reproductive success) at the cost of the parent's ability to invest in other offspring'. Trivers predicted that the sex providing the greater parental investment will become the limiting resource. Individuals of the sex investing less will compete among themselves for mating opportunities, because they can increase their reproductive success through having numerous partners in a way that members of the other sex cannot. Trivers's predictions have been shown to be correct for a wide variety of animals. In most animals, the relative lack of male parental investment leads males to compete among themselves for access to mates via female choice or male-male competition. Therefore, it is the males who tend to be polygamous and hence develop the attractive coloration or the glorious tails or overgrown antlers for combating sexual competitors. Here the male's reproductive effort is heavily skewed towards mating effort rather than parental effort.

Trivers's theory is tellingly supported by the reversal of sex roles in species in which males exhibit unusually high levels of parental investment. Among several species of seahorse, for example, the male receives the eggs of the female and carries them in a pouch until they hatch. The courtship ritual of seahorses is correspondingly reversed, with the female being more brightly coloured and engaging in the more active courtship. Ironically, some people rely on just these sex-reversal cases for the argument that sex roles are arbitrary. However, the theory does not predict that males will be more active in courtship; instead, it predicts that the sex with the smaller parental investment – whether male or female – will be more active.

Male parental investment may take a number of forms, including providing food, defence, a nest, or actual parental care. In humans, the long maturation period of the young meant that ancestral men who tended to provide resources for their mates and children had a reproductive advantage over men who abandoned them and sought other mates.

The relatively large male parental investment notwithstanding, there remains a large sex difference in investment in humans. Even if a man's original mate became pregnant, mating with other women could still enhance his reproductive success. The maximum number of offspring that a man can have is almost limitless, and the minimum investment required from him by each one is small.

By contrast, during gestation the mother cannot become pregnant and therefore cannot directly enhance her reproductive success by additional acts of intercourse; and during lactation pregnancy is much less likely and might decrease the likelihood of the existing child's survival. Therefore, a woman who invested heavily in each child would enjoy greater reproductive success than those mothers who did not. To walk away from the child at birth is to walk away from an investment of nine months' time and tremendous physiological effort.

Thus evolutionary theory predicts different patterns of behaviour for mating specialists and parenting specialists. Mating effort has a high fixed cost; the male must establish himself as successful before he can mate at all. In deer, this entails growing antlers and gaining size; in humans, it may involve acquiring sufficient size and resources to become attractive to a potential mate. These attributes often come much later than the onset of sexual maturity. Once the threshold is crossed, however, the additional investment required to sire a second child may be quite small. But the return on parental effort is different from the return on mating effort, since each additional offspring requires about as much investment as the first. A major consequence of these differences is greater variability in reproductive success in males than in females. Many more males than females will never cross the threshold and have offspring, but the most successful males will have many more offspring than the most successful female. This is true of elephant seals, deer, humans, and most other mammals.

Competition for mates creates winners and losers in the genetic lottery of life, and the greater reproductive variance of males makes the stakes of the game higher for them than for females. Males thus have more to gain by adopting greater risk-taking behaviour (particularly when it comes to acquiring resources and mates), greater aggressiveness, and greater promiscuity. After all, if the male can establish himself as a desirable mate, he may sire many children; if he cannot, he may sire none.

Old head on new shoulders

Choosing a partner, achieving and assessing status, cementing relationships, and correctly identifying off-spring as their own; all these are recurrent adaptive problems faced by our ancestors. Over the last fifteen years there has been a flowering of scholarship produced by 'evolutionary psychologists', who see these functions as performed by the mental tool-box that is our mind. Genes influence our behaviour not by drawing us through life like a puppet on strings of DNA, but by equipping our brains with the tools needed to take in and process the information relevant to solving the problems of our evolutionary past. These mechanisms are not simply 'biological programs' followed without regard to the organism's environment. Rather, they are discrete mental tools that depend on salient environmental inputs to produce adaptive behaviour.

These adaptations forged through tens of thousands of generations constitute our evolutionary heritage – the few generations in a complex industrial society are insignificant in comparison. Therefore, as psychologist

Bruce Ellis has observed, one would 'expect that a man's sexual attractiveness to women will be a function of traits that were correlated with high mate value in our natural environment: the environment of a Pleistocene hunter-gatherer'. One way of seeking an understanding of our nature is to focus on traditional societies, because for most of our evolutionary history we were living in societies rather like these.

In traditional societies, the best predictors of a man's reproductive success are his status and access to resources. Based on a study of almost three hundred mostly non-urban non-Western cultures – where polygyny is the norm – Edgar Gregersen concluded that 'for women the world over, male attractiveness is bound up with social status, or skills, strength, bravery, prowess, and similar qualities'. Anthropologist Laura Betzig, in a far-reaching survey of status and reproductive success, found a high correlation between a man's power and his access to women. As Aristotle Onassis put it: 'If women didn't exist, all the money in the world would have no meaning.'

Some have argued that women's preference for high-status men is not a product of biology but simply a by-product of societal practices that prevent women from securing wealth and status in their own right. If that argument were correct, women's concern with their mates' economic status should decrease as women ascend the economic ladder on their own. The reality is just the opposite; women who have greater economic resources or potential place more importance on a man's economic status than do women with fewer resources. Feminist leaders, no less than other women and perhaps more, desire high-status mates. Moreover, if these desires were motivated solely by the economic concerns of a sexually uniform mind, one would expect that men with fewer resources would value resources in a mate more than would men with greater resources. However, men of low resources and status do not value a potential mate's financial resources any more than financially successful men do.

Evolutionary psychologist David Buss, among others, has shown that modern women are no different from their ancestors in their desire for men of high status, and that modern men are no different from their ancestors in their desire for women exhibiting signals of fertility, such as youth and beauty. Women also favour size and strength in a mate, consistent with the protective function performed by men in the ancestral environment; it is not mere coincidence that height is associated with status in societies around the world. In addition to desiring men who are physically dominant, women also find men with dominant personalities to be far more sexually attractive and desirable as dating partners, while dominance in women is a more neutral trait in men's eyes.

Of course, to say that the traits described – dominance-seeking, nurturing, risk-taking, and so forth – would have been especially valuable to one or the other sex in the past and continue to be valued by potential mates today does not prove that sex differences in these traits actually exist. What follows is a more detailed examination of the differences pertinent to success in the workplace, first establishing whether these differences exist, and then exploring the biological mechanisms that may be responsible.

CHAPTER 2

....

Sex Differences
in Temperament

Evolutionary theory predicts that men will exhibit greater status-seeking, competitiveness, and risk-taking than women, and that women will exhibit more nurturing behaviour. These predictions are borne out in every known human society. It cannot be emphasized too strongly, however, that the differences are statistical, in the sense that they are generalizations that do not hold true for all individuals. There are women who are highly competitive and aggressive, just as there are men averse to competition and more interested in spending time with their children than in ascending hierarchies. But the fact that the predictions are true as generalizations is none the less important. After all, the glass ceiling and the gender gap in compensation are themselves merely group generalizations; many individual women earn more than the average man, and many women ascend higher in the executive ranks than most men. If one wants to say that average temperamental differences are not important because they do not hold true for all individuals, one should also be prepared to say that average economic differences between the sexes are not important for the same reason.

One should also keep in mind that even relatively small between-group differences can have a dramatic effect on the sex ratio at the extremes, and it is the extremes that we are primarily focusing on here. For example, while the average height of men and women in the United States differs by only about six inches – and there are many women who are taller than the average man – the percentage of women among the tallest individuals is vanishingly small. At a height of five-feet-ten, which is approximately the male mean, men outnumber women by approximately 30:1. However, at a height of six feet, men outnumber women by approximately 2,000:1. Thus, an activity where substantial height is required or rewarded will likely be overwhelmingly male, notwithstanding the fact that there are many women who are taller than many men.

Aggressiveness, competitiveness and status-seeking

One of the most consistent differences between the sexes is in 'aggressiveness', a term that can have varying meanings. Psychologists often use the term narrowly to mean inflicting harm on another. However, both psychologists and laymen sometimes define the term more broadly to include not only harm-inflicting behaviour, but also traits such as 'assertiveness', 'competitiveness', 'achievement-motivation', and 'dominance-seeking'. Although not identical, these traits appear to be related.

Among the clearest indicators of disproportionate male aggressiveness is involvement in homicide. Evolutionary psychologists Martin Daly and Margo Wilson have studied homicides around the world and have found a consistent pattern: participants, both perpetrators and victims, are largely unmarried young males. In a study of homicides in Detroit, they found that more than half the cases arose out of 'trivial altercations', either 'escalated showing-off disputes' or 'disputes arising from retaliation for previous verbal or physical abuse'. Daly and Wilson saw both of these forms of homicide as an unequivocal consequence of competitive status-seeking. As biologist Timothy Goldsmith has colourfully noted, '[r]espect of peers is a major determinant of social status, and considering the ever-present hidden agenda that evolutionary history has provided, it is not at all ironic that the proximate goal of the participants in these altercations is to demonstrate that they "have balls".'

Males also exhibit more competitive behaviour and respond more positively than females to competitive situations. While competition significantly increases the motivation of men, it does not do so for women. The more competitive an academic programme is perceived by women, for example, the poorer their performance, while the correlation is reversed for men. Also, when given a choice of tasks to perform, males are likely to select the more difficult task and females the easier one. Females are also more likely to give up after failure and to attribute failure to lack of ability rather than lack of effort. Males, on the other hand, tend to improve in performance after failure.

Males' greater achievement motivation may be related to their greater single-mindedness, a trait that could have substantial ramifications in both the acquisition of skills and the distribution of men and women in the workforce. As psychologist Jacquelynne Eccles has noted, a major dimension of persistence 'is single-minded devotion to one's occupational role' – an 'excessive concern over one's work to the exclusion of other concerns', a pattern that men are much more likely than women to display.

Achievement in mathematics and science reflect these differences in single-mindedness. These are two areas of academic and vocational inequality of contemporary concern, but researchers have found little support for the frequent assertion that males' greater aptitude in these subjects is due entirely to differential socialization. A long-term study of mathematically gifted boys and girls conducted by psychologists Camilla Benbow and David Lubinski showed that boys are much more likely to choose careers in maths and science even though girls are fully aware of their own abilities in these areas. Girls do not have an aversion to maths or science careers but rather simply have broader interests. At one university, for example, scientifically gifted females enrolled in maths and science courses and English and foreign language courses in approximately equal proportions, while males were six times as likely to enrol in maths and science courses than in English and foreign languages. Scientifically gifted boys, it seems, care mostly about science, while gifted girls retain diverse interests.

Males and females also differ substantially in dominance behaviour. Eleanor Maccoby has observed that the male's interest in 'turf and dominance' and the female's interest in maintaining social relationships are visible at an early age. Maccoby attributes the tendency of children to prefer same-sex playmates to this difference in interactive style. This tendency starts as early as age three, and is more marked in unstructured situations than it is in situations structured by adults. She speculates that the orientation of boys towards competition and dominance is aversive to girls, and girls find it difficult to influence boys.

Psychologist Janet Lever observed a number of sex differences in play, including some that are relevant to the workplace. Among the most obvious is the amount of competition exhibited. Lever distinguished between play and games, the former being 'a cooperative interaction that has no explicit goal, no end point, and no winners', and the latter being 'competitive interactions, governed by a set body of rules, and aimed at achieving an explicit known goal'. About 65 per cent of the play activities of boys were formal games, compared to 35 per cent for the girls.

Lever found boys to be far more rule-oriented than girls. Although boys repeatedly quarrelled over the rules, no games were terminated because of such a quarrel, and the boys seemed to enjoy these rule disputes as much as the game. When girls quarrelled over the rules, however, the games often broke up. Boys were also better able than girls to compete against friends and to co-operate with team-mates whom they did not like, and their play was substantially more complex than girls' play.

Girls' play was more social and unstructured, often occurring in private places in small groups and involving the mimicking of primary human relationships, such as hand-holding and 'love notes'. Even when the girls played games, their games were different. Games like hopscotch and jump-rope, for example, are 'turn-taking' games, in which any competition that exists is indirect. When boys competed, they were more likely to compete head-to-head, and because they cared more about winning, their games were always structured so that there would be a clear outcome.

Studies consistently find that girls prefer co-operation to competition and boys prefer competition to co-operation. A marked increase in girls' preference for co-operation over competition comes in the period immediately following puberty, as does an increase in their nurturing behaviour.

Risk-taking

Evolutionary theory also predicts a sex-difference in risk-taking – a behavioural trait relevant to workplace outcomes. Put simply, this is because males have much more to lose in terms of future reproductive success by not taking risks to achieve status, resources and mates. Certainly, the stereotype is that males – especially adolescents and young adults – engage disproportionately in physically risky activity, and psychological studies confirm the stereotype.

Men are disproportionately involved in risky recreational activities such as car racing, sky diving, and hang-gliding. Gambling, risky by definition and design, is a disproportionately male activity, and the higher the stakes the greater the disproportionality becomes. Even when engaged in such mundane activities as sunbathing, males are more likely to take the riskier course of failing to use sunscreen.

The driving style of men also demonstrates a greater propensity towards risk. From the moment they get into the car, more men than women take the risky step of failing to fasten their seatbelts. Once behind the wheel, men suffer far more traffic fatalities than women, not because of their lesser skill in manipulating the vehicle, but because they engage in more risky behaviour, such as speeding, tailgating, refusing to yield the right of way, and running amber lights.

Cross-cultural evidence of male risk-taking activity is abundant. Two of the riskiest activities undertaken in traditional societies – warfare and big-game hunting – are overwhelmingly male activities. A World Health Organization study of accidental death rates for 1971 in fifty countries found a higher death rate for boys in all countries and in all age groups (with the sole exception of one- to four-year-olds in Luxembourg), with the average rate for boys being approximately twice that for girls.

Men's greater willingness to face risks is not limited to physical risks. Psychologist Elizabeth Arch has suggested that sex differences in achievement-orientation may be attributable to differences in risk-taking. From an early age, females are more averse to social, as well as physical, risk, and 'tend to behave in a manner that ensures continued social inclusion'. Arch notes that achievement opportunities often present the potential for loss of resources or group support. Thus, it is not female lack of ability, but rather a difference in attitudes towards failure, that leads women to avoid competitive situations.

Arch's description of male and female attitudes fits easily within an evolutionary framework. She observes that females need explicit positive feedback in order to maintain confidence in themselves, which is an excellent mechanism for ensuring that they will be hesitant to venture into potentially risky situations. In our hunter-gatherer past, this feedback probably came from their kin, with whom they shared some genetic interest. On the other hand, males tend to maintain confidence in themselves despite feedback, 'a response that would be very useful for situations where people challenge and are challenged and where a tendency to face the opponent with a sense of confidence just might provide the margin necessary for victory'.

If in our ancestral environment men could enhance their status – and ultimately their reproductive success – through bluff and bluster, natural selection would have favoured a predisposition to such behaviour. A man hoping to face down a competitor needs to appear confident. Because the best way to convey confidence is actually to have it, natural selection may have favoured a male tendency towards self-deception with regard to their own competencies. On the other hand, since there probably would have been little reproductive pay-off for female competitive behaviours, a propensity towards risk-taking and competitiveness would have been a net disadvantage, given that risk always presents the opportunity for a negative outcome. Thus, a more cautious female approach towards risk and a more conservative assessment of her capacities may have been the more successful strategy.

Nurturing, empathy, and interest in others

Just as men everywhere exhibit more risk-taking and status-seeking behaviour, women everywhere exhibit more nurturing behaviour. Psychologists Eleanor Maccoby and Carol Nagy Jacklin observed that 'women throughout the world and throughout human history are perceived as the more nurturant sex, and are far more likely than men to perform the tasks that involve intimate care-taking of the young, the sick, and the infirm'. Psychologist Carol Gilligan has pointed out that 'women not only define themselves in a context of human relationship but also judge themselves in terms of their ability to care'. Studies routinely show that women are more empathic than men, and their nurturing tendency is present from a very young age and increases at puberty.

Girls tend to be 'person-oriented', while boys tend to be more 'object-oriented'. In one study, subjects were shown pictures of human figures and mechanical objects in a stereoscope so that a human figure and a mechanical object fell simultaneously on the same part of the subject's visual field. The theory behind the experiment is that where two stimuli compete, subjects will attend to the stimulus that is more meaningful to them. Male subjects saw objects more than they saw people, and they saw objects more than did female subjects. Conversely, female subjects saw human stimuli more than they saw objects, and they saw human stimuli more than did male subjects.

As psychologists Katharine and Kermit Hoyenga have observed, women's 'concepts of self are centered more around relationships with others, whereas men's egoistic dominance means that their self-concepts are centered more around task performances and skills'. In one study, for example, 50 per cent of the women but only 15 per cent of the men agreed with the statement, 'I'm happiest when I can succeed at something that will also make other people happy.'

In sum, males and females have grossly different temperamental styles. Men tend to be competitive, while women tend to be more co-operative. Men want to be at the top of a dominance hierarchy, while women seek to cement less-stratified social relations. Men tend to be single-minded in their pursuits, while women have more varied interests. As men and women seem to exhibit the kind of behaviour predicted by evolutionary theory, the next step is to ask whether these manifest differences have their origins in biology, and hence, in genetic differences amenable to natural selection.

CHAPTER 3

....

Are Observed Differences Biologically Based?

An empirical demonstration of temperamental sex differences does not establish that they have a basis in biology. Many argue that they arise from differences in socialization. However, several independent sources suggest that temperamental sex differences do indeed have a biological basis. Evidence from behavioural genetics indicates that many personality traits are highly heritable; that is, much of their individual variation is attributable to genetic differences among individuals. Studies in both humans and animals have shown that sex hormones have a substantial effect on the specific behaviours that we are considering. Studies of infants and young children show that sex-typed behaviour develops at such an early age that an explanation based purely on social conditioning is not plausible. And anthropological evidence shows that many of the sex differences we observe in our society are cross-cultural universals. Taken separately, these bodies of evidence strongly indicate a biological basis for observed sex differences; taken together, they are overwhelming.

Behavioural genetics

The field of behavioural genetics, which attempts to measure the 'heritability' of particular traits, is an important source of evidence for a biological basis for the traits at issue. Heritability is a measure of the portion of trait variation that can be attributed to variation in genetic make-up. The methods of behavioural geneticists vary, but the primary method of estimating the effects of genes and environment is to examine traits in twins and adopted children.

The rationale of twin studies is that identical (or monozygotic) twins are virtually identical genetically, since they result from division of a single fertilized egg. Fraternal (or dizygotic) twins result from fertilization of two eggs by two sperm cells and are no more alike genetically than any other pair of siblings; that is, they share on average 50 per cent of their genes by descent. Comparison of the correlations for a trait between identical and fraternal twins allows an estimate of the magnitude of genetic factors. If identical twins are more similar than same-sex fraternal twins, one may fairly conclude that the trait is influenced by genes. Another method is to compare identical twins reared together with those who were reared apart. If twins reared apart are as similar in a trait as twins reared together, then environmental influences would seem relatively unimportant.

Behavioural geneticists also compare correlations between siblings raised apart and between adopted children and unrelated siblings. If siblings adopted into different homes are more similar to one another than they are to the unrelated children with whom they are reared that would suggest a biological component to the trait. The same is true for a greater correlation between adopted children and their biological parents than between those children and their adoptive parents.

Employing the above techniques, behavioural geneticists have demonstrated substantial genetic contributions to a whole range of personality traits that are relevant to career success. One large-scale study of twins, for example, examined a series of personality dimensions, including 'Social Potency' – which is a measure of dominance – 'Achievement', 'Aggression' and 'Social Closeness'. Heritability estimates for these various dimensions ranged from 0.39 to 0.58, meaning that from 39 to 58 per cent of the variation in these traits is accounted for by genetic differences among individuals.

One counter-intuitive, yet consistent, finding of behavioural geneticists is that shared family environment – at least within the normal range – has little impact on personality similarity in siblings. That is, the important environmental influences seem to be idiosyncratic, either influences outside the home or non-shared family influences, such as birth order or parental favouritism. Shared family influences that are commonly thought to be important – such as the emotional expressiveness of parents, the level of intellectual stimulation in the home, styles of discipline, religious or political beliefs of parents, and socio-economic status – seem to have little impact on developmental outcomes such as intelligence or the 'Big Five' personality dimensions of extraversion, agreableness, conscientiousness, emotional stability and intellectual openness.

The fact that there is a genetic basis for individual differences within a group does not mean that differences between groups necessarily have a genetic basis. For example, it is widely accepted that genes are partially responsible for individual differences in IQ; but this does not in itself demonstrate that genes are responsible for differences in IQ among different racial groups. Thus, heritability studies do not prove a genetic basis for sex differences in personality. However, the studies do show that personality traits are influenced by genes and are therefore subject to natural selection. Evolutionary theory explains why personality traits such as dominance and risk-taking would be valuable to men in our ancestral environment, and we have seen evidence that women preferentially mate with men exhibiting these traits. Once it is seen that these traits have a genetic basis, the picture of how natural selection may have operated becomes more comprehensive.

Hormones and behaviour

An understanding of how sexual differentiation develops in an individual is essential to an understanding of the origin of behavioural sex differences. Males and females begin life almost genetically identical. Both have twenty-two pairs of 'autosomal' chromosomes, which do not differ between the sexes. In addition, the female has two 'X' chromosomes, and the male has one 'X' and one 'Y' chromosome, the latter containing very little genetic material. Thus, except for the redundancy of the X chromosome in females and the small amount of genetic material on the Y chromosome of males, the sexes are genetically identical. Given the similarity of the genetic complement of males and females and the disparity in their biology – particularly reproductive biology – it appears that something major is created by what might at first glance seem to be minor differences between the sexes. That 'something major' is hormones.

Male and female embryos develop identically for approximately the first two months. Thereafter, anatomical and physiological differentiation begins, and the appearance of the sexes begins to diverge. The Y chromosome of the male plays a central role in causing the previously undifferentiated gonad to develop into testes through production of a substance known as 'testis-determining factor'.

Prior to sexual differentiation, the primordial genital tract of both sexes contains three components: (1) undifferentiated gonads; (2) two genital duct systems (the Wolffian system and the Müllerian system); and (3) a common opening for the genital ducts and the urinary tract to the outside. If the foetus is a normal chromosomal male, the testes secrete a substance known as 'Müllerian-inhibiting substance', which causes regression of the Müllerian ducts. If the foetus is a normal chromosomal female, the Müllerian ducts persist and the Wolffian ducts regress. In males, two related androgens – or 'male hormones' – cause development of the male genital tract: testosterone, which virilizes the Wolffian system; and dihydrotestosterone, which virilizes the external genitalia. In the absence of testicular secretions – or if foetal tissues are insensitive to the secretions – a female form occurs, even if the foetus has a Y chromosome. Consequently, the female form is often considered the 'basic' human form.

Just as androgens shape the foetus's sexual anatomy in a male direction, they also shape its brain. During a critical period – probably between sixteen and twenty-eight weeks of gestation – exposure of the brain to androgens results in psychosexual differentiation. Exposure of a chromosomal female to androgens will cause psychological development in the male direction, and absence of androgens in a chromosomal male will cause psychological development in the female direction. The effect of hormones on the developing foetal brain is referred to as the 'organizing effect'. Evidence of the organizing effect of androgens comes primarily from three sources: (1) studies of humans who were exposed as foetuses to atypical endogenous hormones; (2) studies of humans whose mothers were given sex hormones during pregnancy; and (3) animal studies.

One of the best-studied examples of exposure of female foetuses to high levels of androgens is the condition known as congenital adrenal hyperplasia (CAH). Although most androgens come from the male testes, the adrenal glands of both sexes produce small amounts, and therefore low levels of androgens are present in normal female foetuses. CAH results from an excess production of androgens by the foetal adrenal gland, which results from a defect in the synthesis of cortisol, an adrenal hormone.

Exposure of the female CAH foetus to androgens

causes virilization of the external genitalia but it comes too late to cause virilization of the internal reproductive system. At birth, she may have a penis and scrotum (although the scrotum will be empty because the chromosomally female baby produces no testis-determining factor), or she may have an enlarged clitoris and partial fusing of the labia majora. The condition is generally diagnosed at, or soon after, birth. The genitalia are surgically corrected, and the cortisol deficiency is remedied through supplementation. When properly treated, these girls develop as normal fertile females (though often with a delayed onset of menstruation).

CAH girls are of special interest to researchers studying the effects of hormones, because, except for the cortisol deficiency, they are normal girls who were exposed to male hormones *in utero* but raised as girls. The classic studies of these children were conducted by John Money, Anke Ehrhardt, and their colleagues. In comparing CAH girls to matched controls, they found that CAH girls exhibited more stereotypic male behaviour and less stereotypic female behaviour than did controls. Most of the CAH girls considered themselves tomboys throughout their childhood, while none of the control girls did. Only a few of the control girls reported brief episodes of tomboy behaviour, whereas for the CAH girls tomboyism was a way of life.

Corroborative evidence for the hormonal hypothesis comes from the condition known as Androgen Insensitivity Syndrome (AIS). While CAH girls are chromosomal girls who are exposed to high levels of androgens, AIS boys are chromosomal boys whose tissues are insensitive to testosterone; thus, they are in effect subjected to the hormonal environment of a girl. Because their tissues are insensitive to androgens, the Wolffian system never differentiates, and male external genitalia do not develop. At birth, these babies often look like normal females. At puberty, oestrogens, which both males and females produce, cause the development of breasts and pubic hair. The condition is often not diagnosed until the patient fails to menstruate or experiences fertility problems. AIS patients tend to exhibit stereotypically female preferences (such as for being a wife with no outside job) and to be interested in infants and dolls, leading researchers to conclude that hormones, rather than chromosomal sex, are responsible for psychosexual differentiation.

In addition to 'experiments of nature' like CAH and AIS, additional data on pre-natal hormonal exposure come from studies of offspring born to mothers treated with hormones for maintaining high-risk pregnancy. In a comprehensive review of such cases, June Reinisch, then-director of the Kinsey Institute for Research in Sex, Gender, and Reproduction, concluded that the hormone treatments had a substantial masculinizing or feminizing effect, depending upon the hormone given.

Studies conducted on a variety of mammals reveal clearly what human studies merely suggest: exposure to androgens at a critical time in development is crucial to the development of appropriate species-specific male behaviour. These studies show that males who are castrated, either surgically or chemically, prior to the critical period for psychosexual differentiation, develop stereotypic female behaviours. Conversely, exposure of females to androgens during the critical period leads to stereotypic male behaviours.

Sex hormones not only have an organizing effect, they also produce an 'activational effect', which is their immediate influence on behaviour. For example, levels of circulating testosterone are correlated with aggression in adolescents. A study of saliva testosterone levels of prison inmates found higher concentrations in inmates convicted of violent crimes than in those convicted of non-violent crimes. Moreover, comparisons between men showing high and low levels of aggressiveness reveal higher testosterone levels in the more aggressive group. In old age, as the sex-hormone levels of men and women become more similar, sex differences in aggressiveness recede.

In non-human mammals, the activational effect of androgens is clear. For example, injections of testosterone into female monkeys not only increase their aggressive behaviour but also increase their dominance status. Moreover, testosterone injections reduce nurturant behaviour in a variety of species. Even many who question the strength of the evidence of a hormonal contribution to human behaviour acknowledge that the effect is clear in our primate relatives.

The reluctance to invoke biological explanations has led social scientists to rely on socialization as a means of transmitting sex roles. The next chapter will examine why 'learning' alone is not up to the task.

CHAPTER 4

....

The Role of Society

In the current cultural milieu, the burden of proof is assumed to rest on those favouring a biological origin of sex differences. Social constructionists merely assert the social origin of the differences and usually fail to deal with not only the genetic, hormonal, and animal data, but also the cross-cultural uniformity of the differences, clinging tenaciously to the false hope that males and females are different only because we choose to make them so. They point to various societal expectations and stereotypes as proof that the differences are 'socially constructed' – 'society' decided that men should be competitive, aggressive risk-takers and women should be nurturing, co-operative, and less overtly aggressive. However, the existence of societal expectations and stereotypes is not inconsistent with a biological cause. The stereotype that men are taller and stronger than women does not mean that men's greater stature and strength are socially constructed.

Social constructionists also overlook the cross-cultural uniformity of sex differences, a phenomenon difficult to explain without reference to some underlying component of the human psyche. If it occurred through independent invention in each cultural group, why did culture after culture come to the same conclusion? Some arguments have gone to ludicrous extremes to marginalize the role of biology.

Biologist Anne Fausto-Sterling suggests that the universality of sex differences may be attributed to the fact that 'the entire population of the world all evolved from a small progenitor stock and these behaviors have been faithfully passed down [culturally] from generation to generation a thousand times over'. Her argument itself necessarily rests on assumptions concerning the human psyche and raises further questions. First, why did the progenitor group decide on the initial 'rules'? This group was not transplanted from another planet fully formed; the 'progenitor stock' had its own biological progenitors in an ape-like primate, which almost certainly already exhibited its own sex differences. Second, how can one square the faithfulness with which this 'cultural artifact' has been transmitted from generation to generation with its being simply an arbitrary choice? To explain these traits on the basis of 'universally common socialization processes', as Fausto-Sterling does, is to provide no explanation at all. A more likely solution would be that there is something in our nature that leads us consistently to the same answer.

The early appearance of many sex differences also

makes their social origins suspect. Children develop sex-typed preferences before they learn sex-role stereotypes, and they exhibit same-sex playmate preferences before they can reliably identify which children are the same sex as themselves. As Eleanor Maccoby has pointed out, an innate bias towards same-sex play is suggested by the fact that the same sex-segregation appears in non-human primates 'among whom the cultural transmission of cognitive gender stereotypes is surely minimal'.

This is not to say that social inputs are completely irrelevant. Children may internalize sex-appropriate behaviour in part from observation of the world around them and reinforcement of those behaviours. However, one wonders how parents and schools that consciously attempt to avoid sex-stereotyping keep producing children with the same basic ideas. To say that the children 'pick up subtle cues from the world around them' is an incomplete answer. Unless children are biologically 'programmed' to internalize sex roles in much the same way they are 'programmed' to acquire language, it is difficult to see why they do it so readily. As psychiatrist Isaac Marks has observed, '[a]ll species learn some things far more easily than they do others, a facility shaped by natural selection'.

The fact that children may absorb certain lessons readily does not mean that they will absorb all lessons equally readily. For example, many parents struggle mightily against the sibling rivalry of their children to no avail. It is simply very difficult to cause children to view parental investment directed towards their siblings as being just as valuable as parental investment directed towards themselves. Because human groups generally are made up of individuals with conflicting interests, a propensity for absorbing cultural information uncritically would leave one vulnerable to exploitation in the reproductive interests of others.

Even a showing that appropriate sex-typed behaviour is explicitly taught by parents does not suggest that we have moved completely from the realm of evolved psychology into the realm of culture. Human parents are not alone in teaching their offspring, and human children are not alone in imitating their parents. Such patterns are seen in many species. It seems quite probable that when parents differentially reinforce behaviours in boys and girls they are acting in accordance with their own evolved psychological mechanisms. For example, Bobbi Low has shown that in polygynous societies, where the potential reproductive pay-off of male competition is highest, parents train their boys to be especially competitive.

Perhaps the closest approximation to a laboratory test of the socialization hypothesis comes from the Israeli kibbutzim, which were studied by anthropologists Lionel Tiger and Joseph Shepher. The kibbutz movement was founded in 1910 upon an ideology similar to that of many modern feminists: a necessary and sufficient condition of women's emancipation is the elimination of sex roles and the liberation of women from domestic obligations. Kibbutz ideology attributed sexual inequality to the 'biological tragedy of women', which caused women to be economically dependent upon men and shackled to the domestic sphere.

Collective socialization replaced maternal care in the kibbutz. Children lived in age-graded children's houses;

and communal kitchens, laundries, and dining rooms were created to relieve women of housekeeping duties. Men and women were free to seek the work they chose, and equal participation in the political sphere was expected.

From the beginning, however, most positions of authority were held by men. A one-third minimum quota for women in the governing bodies of one of the kibbutz federations was seldom met because so few women were willing to serve. Notwithstanding the ideology, neither the sexual division of labour nor other aspects of sex roles disappeared for long. Although in the early years, work filled a role in the life of women nearly equivalent to that of men, by the 1950s men were doing farming, the highest-status occupation in the kibbutz, and women were acting as nurses and teachers. Laundry and cooking were still done by women, whose jobs were in the service sector. Whereas their grandmothers sought to minimize sexual dimorphism, the granddaughters found a new interest in fashion and jewellery. Parents, especially mothers, grew increasingly dissatisfied with the practice of collective sleeping for the children. The emotional centrality of family increased for women, so that women came to view caring for their children as an important source of fulfilment. This 'reversion to type' continues into the present, and sex-role distinctions are greater within the kibbutz than without.

The kibbutz experiment suggests that sex roles, assumed by many to be mere cultural artifacts, have much deeper origins. Members of the kibbutzim did not revert to traditional sex roles because they rejected the idea of sexual equality; both men and women continued to profess a belief in equality. Instead, they reverted to traditional roles because they found them more fulfilling.

Men and women differ in fundamental ways consistent with evolutionary predictions. Men are more inclined to take risks, more oriented towards attainment of status and resources, and more single-minded in achieving these goals. Women, on the other hand, are more nurturing and empathic, and more centred on maintaining a 'web' of relationships than on being at the top of a hierarchy. The next chapter will explore what effect these sex differences have on workplace outcomes.

CHAPTER 5

The Modern Workplace

The glass-ceiling metaphor is misleading: it describes a result in the guise of describing a process. It is undeniably true that women are not proportionally represented at the very highest levels in business hierarchies. It is less obviously true that women's under-representation is a consequence of flaws within these organizations, and even less obvious that modification of organizations informed by the false premises of standard social science will eliminate the major part of the differential.

It is a common observation – sometimes a complaint – that in order for women to attain the highest levels in the working world they must 'be like men'. Prominent among the qualities of successful executives of both sexes are the 'male' traits of aggressiveness, ambition and drive, strong career orientation, and risk-taking. Even apart from commitment to children, women as a group differ in important ways from men. Combined with their greater commitment to families these temperamental differences have a powerful effect.

Personality type and career achievement are strongly related. Psychologist Bruce Ellis reports that studies of personality and leadership show that those who rise to the top in organizations 'tend to be bright, initiating, self-assured, decisive, masculine, assertive, persuasive, and ambitious'. One study found that the more 'masculine' the woman, the greater her career achievement. Masculine traits included assertiveness, competitiveness, dominance, and standing up well under pressure, while feminine traits included nurturing, accommodating warmth, and eagerness to soothe hurt feelings. Career achievement was positively correlated with masculinity and negatively correlated with femininity. Interestingly, whether a woman was classified as masculine or feminine was unrelated to her marital status or fertility.

The sex differences in attitudes towards risk discussed in Chapter 2 cannot help but have an impact on work-force distributions. Women often gravitate to lower career-risk positions. The 1995 Glass Ceiling Commission found that most female professionals and managers do not work in the private for-profit sector, but rather hold jobs in the public or non-profit sectors, which tend not only to be less risky but also often offer more regular hours and may be more likely to involve a 'caring' profession. Women managers are more likely to be found in staff positions – such as human resources, corporate communications, and community and government relations – than in line positions, such as running a factory or a division. Line positions carry higher risk because success or failure is more easily determined and more directly related to corporate profits. Staff positions and positions in the public and non-profit sector, on the other hand, tend to carry with them lower career risk, less pressure to relocate, and fewer irregular hours.

Studies of successful executives regularly find that willingness to take risks is one of the primary attributes that sets them apart from others. In a study of top executives, researchers found a consistent picture: 'a higher degree of success (i.e., wealthier, higher income, higher position, more authority) differentiated the risk-takers from the risk averters'. The researchers suggest that for 'most businesses, a person gets to the top by taking risks and having them work out for the best'. The downside of risk, of course, is that by definition many risk-takers, a disproportionate number of whom are males, end up as losers.

Although sex differences in motivation appear to be in part a function of differences in risk preference, that is not the whole story. Also important is the willingness to make the commitment of time and energy that is required to break into the executive ranks. When a Fortune 500 company was sued for discrimination for not hiring enough women managers, it commissioned a study to determine the reasons. The study concluded that the disparity in promotion rates 'reflected differences in behaviors and attitudes of male and female clerks – differences the company and its policies had no part in producing'. Among the differences in attitudes were women's being significantly less willing than men to relocate for promotion or to work longer hours, and less inclined to view their jobs as stepping stones to higher positions. This is not to suggest, of course, that these preferences exist wholly apart from other features of the labour market. Rather, the motivations of the women must be understood in context. For example, part of the reason for a woman's lesser willingness to relocate may be that her husband's job is considered of primary importance, perhaps, but not necessarily, because he earns more. However, these tendencies exist whether or not women have families. It is not surprising that women, who value their web of social relationships more highly than do men, would be more reluctant than men to relocate to a place where they do not know anyone. In any event, employers must deal with the actual preferences of their employees, whatever their cause.

The study revealed that the largest sex difference was between highly motivated married men and highly motivated married women. Among the former, marriage increased promotion-seeking behaviour, while among the latter it decreased it, a finding that has been widely replicated. The presence of children further exaggerated these differences. The study concluded that the lower promotion rates of women were not due to discrimination but rather to differences in motivation: 'those women who are prepared to seek and accept responsibility are promoted like men who behave in the same way'.

The glass ceiling?

If the 'glass ceiling' is caused in part by women's displaying fewer of the temperamental traits and accompanying behaviours that result in achievement, then for women to achieve parity either the job requirements or women themselves must change. Many have advocated both changes: employers should stop rewarding driven and ambitious people, and girls should be socialized to manifest the same drive and ambition as males (or, conversely, boys should be socialized out of their dominance-seeking and aggressiveness). For a host of reasons, neither of these suggestions is likely to bear fruit.

It is unlikely that employers will cease rewarding employees who exhibit a high degree of commitment to the employer. All else being equal – and in the absence of legal prohibition – an employer will generally prefer a worker who puts in more hours to one who puts in fewer; who will travel or relocate to one who will not; and whose career is not interrupted by lengthy absences from the labour market to one whose is.

If employers' values are not modified, then parity might be achieved by making women more like men. Many have advocated 'sex-free' socialization and an end to 'sexist' child rearing for just this reason. As we have seen, however, socialization is far less important than is commonly recognized, and there seems little reason to think that we will be much more successful in eliminating the differences than the kibbutzniks were.

The focus on achievements of males and females as groups should not obscure the fact that just as most women do not rise to the top of the pyramid, neither do most men. High executive positions are scarce, and the men who hold them had to compete against other men to get them. The Glass Ceiling Commission seemed oblivious to this fact. It quoted one woman as complaining, 'If I want to succeed I have to accept the white male notion of what constitutes the good life. But even when we do that and demonstrate excellent performance by their standards, it doesn't guarantee a trip to the top.' The woman is certainly correct that even excellent performance does not 'guarantee a trip to the top'. But it doesn't do so for either sex; no one who understands the business world would think otherwise.

Although comparable men and women enjoy comparable economic outcomes in the workplace, they may not enjoy comparable psychological outcomes. The life-satisfaction that a successful career brings to a man does not necessarily come to a woman. In one study of men and women engineers, for example, there was a significant positive correlation between work and non-work satisfaction in men but not in women.

The male desire for status is in large part biological, and our biology is not changing at a perceptible rate. Similarly, a major reason for women's lack of single-minded devotion to career is their commitment to their children. This is also a product of our evolutionary heritage, and the notion that women will in large numbers completely overlook their children in favour of their careers is no more realistic than the notion that one can have a completely satisfying high-powered career and be fully involved with the lives of one's children.

It might be argued that even if strong sex differences exist between young men and young women, such differences cannot explain differential representation of the sexes in the top executive ranks, because people generally do not achieve those positions until they are in their late forties or fifties, by which time men and women have become more hormonally similar and women may no longer have children at home who need their attention. However, such an argument ignores the fact that the career trajectory is set much earlier, and the ladder to the top typically takes twenty to twenty-five years to ascend. Thus, career outcomes in middle age are closely related to career investment in the younger years.

The 'glass ceiling' metaphor may be backwards. The metaphor describes imperceptible barriers that prevent women from reaching the executive suite. Perhaps a more apt metaphor would be the 'gossamer ceiling' – a barrier that women 'see' but that is not strong enough to hold back those who choose to cross it.

The gender gap in compensation

The term 'gender gap' refers to the fact that full-time female employees on average earn approximately three-quarters what full-time male employees earn. Like the glass ceiling, the gender gap is a group-based phenomenon. Women whose productivity-related traits and occupational choices are similar to men's tend to be compensated like men, but women as a group earn less than men because of differences in qualifications and occupational choices.

Many of the differences contributing to the gender gap are just what evolutionary theory would predict. Full-time female employees work fewer hours than full-time male employees. Economist Victor Fuchs has reported that among white women with eighteen years or more of schooling and at least one child under twelve at home, only one in ten works more than 2,250 hours per year; in contrast, half the husbands of those women work that many hours. Just as working fewer hours impedes advancement, it also causes lower earnings. Also, women leave the labour force at a much higher rate than men do, and even a temporary hiatus may have a significant effect on earnings years later.

Men and women also differ in the job features they favour. Wages are not paid simply for hours of labour but rather for hours of labour doing a particular job. Thus, wages are in part compensation for disagreeable aspects of the job, such as physical risk. If two jobs are otherwise identical but one carries with it a substantial risk of injury, for example, the risky job will carry a higher rate of pay. Attitudes towards risk, which are not random with respect to sex, have economic consequences. It is not a coincidence that occupations exposing workers to the greatest risk of death are largely male, or that males account for over 90 per cent of workplace deaths in the United States.

The relevance of attitudes towards risk is not limited to physical risk. Men are more likely than women to choose fields entailing 'career risk', meaning that success is possible but not guaranteed. In accordance with the general rule that with greater risk comes the possibility of greater rewards, a study of female executive compensation revealed that ambition and willingness to take risk are positively related to compensation.

Men and women also exhibit systematic differences in the value that they place on other job features. Men attach more importance to financial aspects of the job, while women value various interpersonal and other non-wage aspects of the job, such as safer working conditions, flexibility of hours, shorter commute time, and opportunity to help others, preferences that may account for the concentration of women in public-sector jobs. For both men and women, those individuals who place a high personal priority on earnings tend to earn more than those who assign less importance to financial success and more importance to other job attributes.

Differences in preferences are found even within occupations. Among physicians, women are less likely to specialize, and when they do they often concentrate in low-prestige specialities. Men are more likely to be in private practice, while women are more likely to be salaried employees in non-entrepreneurial settings. Even within specialities these differences hold. Among obstetrician/gynaecologists, for example, women are more likely than men to work in salaried positions with regular (and lower) hours, and men are more oriented towards higher incomes and private practice. Consistent with data from other studies, the presence of children in the home increases the number of work hours for male obstetricians and decreases the number for females.

Tests of vocational interest consistently reveal sex differences, and these differences have economic ramifications. At least since the days of Adam Smith, students of labour markets have understood that wage differentials across industries are explicable in part by the nature of working conditions. Economist Randall Filer has concluded that a substantial portion of the wage gap is caused by the fact that men take jobs that are less attractive than those filled by women, or, put another way, 'by differentials paid by women in order to obtain more attractive jobs'.

The lesser attractiveness of many men's jobs tends to be obscured in the discussion of occupational segregation and work-force equality. Admittedly, jobs carrying the very highest status tend to be occupied by men, and many of the jobs carrying the lowest wages are occupied by women. But these two data do not tell the whole story. On average, jobs held by women are rated as slightly higher in status than jobs held by men, because, although men hold the highest-status jobs, they also hold the lowest ones. Moreover, although women hold many of the lowest-paying jobs, men have a virtual monopoly on the least attractive jobs. Warren Farrell has pointed out that twenty-four of the twenty-five 'worst' jobs as rated in *The Jobs Rated Almanac* (judged on a combination of salary, stress, work environment, outlook, security, and physical demands) were 95 to 100 per cent male; the twenty-fifth job was equally male and female.

The simplistic observation that men and women have different average earnings is misleading. As economist Jennifer Roback has noted, '[o]nce we observe that people sacrifice money income for other pleasurable things we can infer next to nothing by comparing the income of one person with another.' However, the fact that earnings are easier to quantify than other job attributes leads to an undue focus on compensation disparities. If women make the same kinds of human-capital investments and occupational choices as men, their compensation will be similar to men's. If women choose to work fewer hours, seek less job-related training, and select jobs with advantages that for them outweigh the lower pay, they will earn less.

CHAPTER 6

....

Feminism and the Status of Women in the Workplace

The feminist literature on the status of women in the workplace starts from the premise that the glass ceiling and the gender gap in compensation are indicators of 'disadvantage'. If representation at the top of employment hierarchies and compensation levels are the only measures of advantage, then women are indeed disadvantaged. These two factors alone, however, do not provide a complete picture.

Most feminists acknowledge that a major reason that women do not receive equal extra-domestic outcomes is that they have opted for a larger measure of satisfaction in the domestic sphere. Women invest more than men domestically and get more in return, and they invest less extra-domestically and get less in return. Self-esteem of men is much more closely related to occupational success than is the self-esteem of women, which is more tied to success in social relationships. In sum, the sexes have different definitions of success in life.

One of the primary reasons that men hold a disproportionate number of the highest-paying jobs is that they have a greater commitment to the labour market. Women care less about climbing hierarchies and about objective forms of recognition such as money, status, and power than men. They place more importance on a high level of involvement with their children. These conclusions are consistent with evolutionary theory, biological fact, and psychological data. It is simply the case that women tend to fit work to families, while men fit families to work.

If women are less willing to sacrifice family for career, one might characterize their decisions as the product of free choice. But rather than celebrate the fact that a woman can choose to nurture her children, a common response of feminists is to deny that there is any choice at all; at best there is a forced 'choice'. Why are these not real choices? For two reasons: first, because the range of choices is substantially restricted; second, because it is usually the woman, rather than the man, who makes the choice to forsake career for family. Both of these observations are empirically true, but neither demonstrates that the decisions are not choices.

Our options are always limited. We must constantly make trade-offs based upon our own priorities; that we prefer A to B does not mean that our selection of A is not a free choice. The different trade-offs of the sexes simply demonstrate that they have different priorities. The fact that these choices are influenced by biology does not make them any less choices.

The common observation that women must choose between career and family, while men need not, rests on the false premise that men do not make trade-offs between family and career. On the contrary, stories of male executives who seldom see their children are a commonplace. The woman who has sufficient capacity and desire for a high-powered career can pursue it and still 'have a family', just as a man can.

The assertion that women cannot have a high-powered career and a family is based upon a sexual asymmetry in what is meant by 'having a family'. A male executive who has a wife who does not work outside the home and who seldom sees his children is considered to 'have it all' – career and family. Even if his wife works and his children are in day care all day, he still 'has it all'. The female executive – perhaps the wife of the male executive described above – who seldom sees her children is seen as having sacrificed family for career. She does not 'have it all', even if she has exactly what her husband has.

The reason that the model of the absentee mother is not deemed acceptable rests on a sex difference in what it means to 'have a family'. For many women (and more women than men), it means spending substantial time nurturing children. This difference is reflected in the linguistic distinction between 'fathering a child' and 'mothering a child', the former meaning contributing to conception and the latter meaning contributing to ongoing care. A father demonstrates his commitment to his family by working, while a mother demonstrates her commitment by providing direct care. The phrase 'having a family' has different meanings for the two sexes. Only by failing to recognize that fact is it possible to argue that women are asking only for what men already have.

If no systematic difference existed between the choices of men and women, the fact that people who devote more time and energy to their career receive greater career rewards would not be a problem. Most people would probably be shocked to learn of a proposal requiring equal rewards for different levels of career investment; but that is precisely the proposal that many feminists make. The labour market is criticized for rewarding high levels of commitment on the theory that to do so disadvantages women, but it disadvantages women only to the extent that individual women choose not to invest, and it disadvantages individual men on the same basis.

It is ironic that feminists seize on the lack-of-choice argument, since women have a much broader range of work/family choices than men do. A woman can choose to be a 'career primary' worker, a 'career and family' worker, a part-time worker, or a full-time housewife; all of these are socially respected choices. Men, on the other hand, have little choice at all. They are expected to be full-time workers who, in most circumstances, are the primary family breadwinners.

Some feminists argue that we need to 'change the paradigm' – that societal expectations should be broad enough to encompass the 'house husband' model. If society were only willing to give its imprimatur, then half the primary breadwinners would be women and half the homemakers would be men. An understanding of evolutionary psychology reveals the naivety of the belief that many families would choose that model. Men's desire for status and tangible rewards is biologically ingrained and runs deeper than a mere social 'paradigm', as is women's desire for high-status men. The notion that large numbers of female executives and professionals would be willing to marry men who would stay home and tend the children is nothing short of fanciful. Successful women not only want husbands who work, they – to a much greater extent than men – want mates who are also highly successful. It will be the rare man who is willing to stay home with the children and be supported by his wife for an extended period, and it will be the rarer wife who is willing to support such a husband and who finds such a man sexually attractive. Suggestions that 'men just need to change' will be no more fruitful and are no more appropriate than suggestions that women should.

Instead of identifying women as the victims of current arrangements, one could as easily view men as being the disadvantaged sex. Because of their drive for status and resources and the interest of women in such attributes in potential mates, men choose more money, little time with family, longer hours, and unpleasant working conditions. The large number of men willing to make such choices has given employers an ample supply of striving employees, but, of course, if men were not willing to play the game, employers could not demand it.

The price that men pay for what their competitiveness earns them is not limited to decreased domestic participation. The competitive, testosterone-driven nature of men that drives them to seek status and resources also drives them to an early grave. Like almost all mammals, the human male has a lesser life expectancy than the female. Psychologist Marianne Frankenhaeuser has suggested that the greater vulnerability of men to coronary heart disease may be related to the male's 'more intense and more frequent neuroendocrine stress responses in response to achievement demands'. However, this is not viewed as a social problem, and there are no public-policy initiatives to close the 'life-expectancy gap'.

It is worth noting that one unfortunate consequence of the feminists' denial of the reality of choice is its implicit denigration of the domestic role, since it assumes that housewives are oppressed victims, that women fill that role only because they are forced into it or too gullible to realize that it is not in their interest. This places women in a position in which there is little chance of winning. If the role of wife and mother carries a high status, women may achieve status by adopting it. However, if high-status roles are found exclusively in the extra-domestic sphere – a sphere in which men's temperament gives them an advantage – then women will be forever consigned to lower status.

CONCLUSION

Men and women are different. They have on average different temperaments, priorities, and definitions of success. These differences are produced in substantial measure by underlying psychological differences that were adaptive in our evolutionary past. The sex differences we see in Western society are replicated both in other societies and, in many cases, throughout the mammalian world. They are products of natural selection, mediated by the interaction of hormones and the brain, and not simply creations of Western civilization, capitalism, or industrialism.

The argument that sex roles have been imposed by society on female victims is inadequate; if current arrangements are the product of choices made by men and women predisposed to make choices in a particular way, arguments that society must remedy the injustice it has visited on women are based upon an erroneous premise of societal culpability.

Pressuring fathers into greater domestic roles, a favourite prescription of many feminists, is unlikely to result in an overall gain in life satisfaction, and it may not even benefit women. Women may say they want more help around the house, but forcing a man to trade extra-domestic success – his primary source of self-esteem – for domestic contributions may cause him to be less satisfied with both his work and his marriage. Conversely, pressuring women to accept management positions that they really do not want is likely to lead to inadequate performance or unwanted stress and changes in family life. These results are likely to be negative for men, women, and children.

Temperamental sex differences will affect workplace outcomes whether or not there are children to be cared for. As the kibbutz experience showed, these differences cause sex roles to persist even when women are relieved of child-care responsibilities. Although freeing up time for a woman may give her more hours to devote to her career if she chooses, she will still be a woman, less competitive and single-minded – on average – than men. Men are competitive risk-takers to an extent that women are not, irrespective of whether they are parents. This does not mean, of course, that individual women who are competitive and single-minded should not have the freedom to pursue high-powered careers. It does, however, suggest that we should not be surprised when women and men sort themselves differently in the workplace.

It simply cannot be seriously argued that sex differences in behaviour in the labour market and in marriage are wholly attributable to features of the labour market or the institution of marriage. After all, men and women often choose different leisure activities when they are wholly unconstrained by employer preferences. Similarly, the fact that husbands generally do less housework than their wives is often taken as a sign that marriage is oppressive to women. However, it should be noted that even prior to marriage women devote more hours to housekeeping than do men, although the disparity is not as great as it is for married men and women.

The thrust of much of the feminist literature is that men and women should come to be more alike. Usually, the suggestion is that men should become more like women: we need to tame the aggressiveness, competitiveness, and risk-taking nature of the male. However, many of the greatest human achievements have been possible only through the kind of single-minded devotion and willingness to take risks that men disproportionately display. Scientific achievements are often a consequence of a consuming obsession. Perhaps not coincidentally, studies of scientific productivity show that on average men publish substantially more than women, whether or not the women have children. Entrepreneurial geniuses exhibit the same sort of work ethic and risk-taking nature as scientific geniuses. A study of such people found that they shared the following attributes: autocratic, charismatic, competitive, confident, driven, focused, impatient, intuitive, passionate, persistent, persuasive, rebellious, and risky.

Sometimes the converse suggestion is made: we need to make females more like males, for example by increasing their preference for risk. The fact that risk-taking propensities have roots in our evolved psychologies does not mean they cannot be modified at all. One should not overlook the disadvantages of risk, however. The focus of this book has been on workplace success and therefore has provided a somewhat one-sided view of risk. Successful executives are usually people who have taken risks and won, but by definition many risk-takers lose. Modifying the relative values that women place on success and failure may increase the number of women who succeed spectacularly, but it would also surely increase the number of spectacular failures.

Much of the disagreement over the status of women in the workplace is a philosophical one: should social policy focus on groups or on individuals? Current workplace arrangements are largely a result of individual choices of men and women guided by their own psyches. The question is whether the choices are rendered suspect – if not illegitimate – by group differences in the choices made. The fact that some people prefer to focus their energies on their families while others prefer to concentrate on their careers is not the perceived problem. Instead, the demand for social intervention arises because the former group is disproportionately female, while the latter group is disproportionately male. Similarly, the fact that the business world rewards competitive risk-takers is not by itself a problem; the problem is that risk-takers tend to be men.

At bottom, much of the feminist case is based upon a normative vision of what women should want, rather than on what they do want. To deny the existence of choice because of the way it is exercised is ultimately an authoritarian response. In a very real sense, the patterns we now see are themselves a product of female choice; over thousands of generations, women have chosen men who display the traits that many feminists now claim to disdain.

Many of the feminist arguments are plagued by a fundamental inconsistency. They reject the male obsession with status, competition, and acquisition of resources, but they measure women's position in society solely along this male dimension. They then conclude that women are disadvantaged without incorporating into their measurement the attributes that women value.

Despite a level of complaint that would suggest otherwise, most women do not feel disadvantaged. Surveys show that women are generally happy with their lives and with their jobs – indeed no less satisfied with their jobs than men. These findings are consistent with the view that the workplace/family accommodations they have reached are satisfying to them. It should be noted that despite feminist arguments that women are perceived as inferior, existing research shows that the popular perception of women is more positive overall than that of men.

A fresh approach

Proponents of social construction have been extremely successful in preventing the biological explanation of differences from affecting public-policy discussions. They have had this success only because of a gross asymmetry in burdens of proof. Without convincing evidence of their own, social constructionists have been permitted to shift the burden to those favouring a biological explanation simply by invoking the concept of 'socialization'. If social-construction explanations had faced the same scepticism that biological explanations face, they could not have persisted as they have.

In evaluating competing claims about the origins of human behaviour, the question should not be whether those finding answers in biology can prove their case to a certainty. The important question should be whether the explanation offered here – that genuine and deep-seated differences between the sexes are a substantial cause of current workplace arrangements – is a more plausible account than the social-constructionists have provided. It is hoped that those who still have doubts concerning the biological explanation will bring the same degree of scepticism, and the same demand for rigorous proof, to the purely sociological explanations.

Many people resist a biological perspective of human nature out of fear that such a perspective will, regardless of its factual basis, produce adverse social consequences. A socialization perspective, they believe, is more in accordance with liberal notions of human autonomy and dignity. There is seldom any articulated basis, however, for the view that a Utopian vision of human perfectibility poses less danger than a vision of humans as organisms with the same kind of 'nature' that we have always understood other species to possess. Indeed, as Noam Chomsky has observed, the notion of the human mind as *tabula rasa* is a powerful tool in the hands of a totalitarian: 'If people are, in fact, malleable and plastic beings with no essential psychological nature, then why should they not be controlled and coerced by those who claim authority, special knowledge, and a unique insight into what is best for those less enlightened?'

The belief that the sexes are identical has led to a number of policies of doubtful wisdom and effectiveness. Employers are pressured to eliminate statistical disparities in their work forces even at the cost of productivity; schools have been converted into organs of propaganda for the message of sexual sameness, without regard to the loss of credibility that may flow from information so at variance with children's own experience; military readiness has been seriously compromised, according to many, by the admission of women into almost all positions and the changes in standards that have been necessary to accomplish that end.

The time has come to move the debate to a different and more fruitful level. While a biological perspective dictates neither whether change is appropriate nor what policies should be adopted to effect desired change, it can inform both of those questions. Policy makers can attempt to move with the grain of human nature or against it, but they are more likely to arrive at successful solutions by modifying the environment to work with human nature than by attempting the impossible task of altering human nature itself.

SUGGESTIONS FOR FURTHER READING

....

INTRODUCTION

Brown, Donald E., *Human Universals*, New York: McGraw-Hill (1991).

Browne, Kingsley R., 'Sex and temperament in modern society: A Darwinian view of the glass ceiling and the Gender Gap', *Arizona Law Review* 37(4), 971–1106 (1995).

CHAPTER 1: Sex Differences and Evolutionary Theory

Betzig, Laura, *Despotism and Differential Reproduction: A Darwinian View of History*, New York: Aldine de Gruyter (1986).

Buss, David M., *The Evolution of Desire: Strategies of Human Mating*, New York: BasicBooks (1994).

Cronin, Helena, *The Ant and the Peacock: Altruism and Sexual Selection from Darwin to Today*, Cambridge: Cambridge University Press (1991).

Darwin, Charles, *The Origin of Species* (1859).

Darwin, Charles, *The Descent of Man, and Selection in Relation to Sex* (1871).

Daly, Martin and Wilson, Margo, *Sex, Evolution and Behavior* (2nd ed.), Belmont, CA: Wadsworth (1983).

Dawkins, Richard, *The Selfish Gene* (new ed.), New York: Oxford University Press (1989).

Diamond, Jared, *The Third Chimpanzee: The Evolution and Future of the Human Animal*, New York: HarperCollins (1992).

Fisher, Helen, *Anatomy of Love: The Mysteries of Mating, Marriage, and Why We Stray*, New York: Norton (1992).

Gilligan, Carol, *In a Different Voice: Psychological Theory and Women's Development*, Cambridge, MA: Harvard University Press (1982).

Goldsmith, Timothy H., *The Biological Roots of Human Nature: Forging Links Between Evolution and Behavior*, New York: Oxford University Press (1991).

Gregersen, Edgar, *Sexual Practices: The Story of Human Sexuality*, New York: F. Watts (1982).

Pinker, Steven, *How the Mind Works*, New York: Norton (1997).

Ridley, Matt, *The Red Queen: Sex and the Evolution of Human Nature*, New York: Macmillan (1993).

Symons, Donald, *The Evolution of Human Sexuality*, New York: Oxford University Press (1979).

Trivers, Robert L., 'Parental investment and sexual selection', in Campbell, Bernard G. (ed.), *Sexual Selection and the Descent of Man*, Chicago: Aldine de Gruyter, pp. 136–179 (1972).

Trivers, Robert L., *Social Evolution*, Menlo Park, CA: Benjamin/Cummings (1985).

Wright, Robert, *The Moral Animal: The New Science of Evolutionary Psychology*, New York: Pantheon (1994).

CHAPTER 2: Sex Differences in Temperament

Arch, Elizabeth C., 'Risk-taking: A motivational basis for sex differences', *Psychological Reports*, 73(1), 3–11 (1993).

Daly, Martin and Wilson, Margo, *Homicide*, New York: Aldine de Gruyter (1988).

Eccles, Jacquelynne S., 'Gender roles and achievement patterns: An expectancy value perspective', in Reinisch, June M. *et al.* (eds.), *Masculinity/Femininity: Basic Perspectives*, New York: Oxford University Press, pp. 240–280 (1987).

Goldberg, Steven, *Why Men Rule: A Theory of Male Dominance*, Chicago: Open Court (1993).

Halpern, Diane, *Sex Differences in Cognitive Abilities* (2nd ed.), Hillsdale, NJ: Lawrence Erlbaum (1992).

Hoyenga, Katharine B. and Hoyenga, Kermit T., *Gender-Related Differences: Origins and Outcomes*, Boston: Allyn & Bacon (1993).

Lever, Janet, 'Sex differences in the games children play', *Social Problems*, 23(4), 478–487 (1976).

Lubinski, David and Benbow, Camilla P., 'Gender differences in abilities and preferences among the gifted: Implications for the math-science pipeline', *Current Directions in Psychological Science*, 1(2), 61–66 (1992).

Maccoby, Eleanor E. and Jacklin, Carolyn N., *The Psychology of Sex Differences*, Stanford, CA: Stanford University Press (1974).

CHAPTER 3: Are Observed Differences Biologically Based?

LeVay, Simon, *The Sexual Brain*, Cambridge, MA: MIT Press (1993).

Moir, Anne, and Jessel, David, *Brain Sex: The Real Difference Between Men and Woman*, New York: Dell (1989).

Money, John, and Ehrhardt, Anke, *Man & Woman: Boy & Girl*, Baltimore, MD: Johns Hopkins University Press (1972).

Plomin, Robert, *Nature and Nurture: An Introduction to Human Behavioral Genetics*, Pacific Grove, CA: Brooks/Cole (1990).

Pool, Robert, *Eve's Rib: The Biological Roots of Sex Differences*, New York: Crown (1994).

Reinisch, June M. *et al.*, 'Hormonal contributions to sexually dimorphic behavioral development in humans', *Psychoneuroendocrinology*, 16(1–3), 213–278 (1991).

Rowe, David C., *The Limits of Family Influence: Genes, Experience, and Behavior*, New York: Guilford Press (1994).

CHAPTER 4: The Role of Society

Fausto-Sterling, A., *Myths of Gender: Biological Theories About Women and Men*, (2nd ed.), New York: Basic Books (1992).

Low, Bobbi S., 'Cross-cultural patterns in the training of children: An evolutionary perspective', *Journal of Comparative Psychology*, 103(4), 311–319 (1989).

Tiger, Lionel, and Shepher, Joseph, *Women in the*

Kibbutz, New York: Harcourt Brace Jovanovich (1975).

CHAPTER 5: The Modern Workplace

Ellis, Bruce J., 'The evolution of sexual attraction: evaluative mechanisms in women', in Barkow, Jerome H., Cosmides, Leda and Tooby, John (eds.), *The Adapted Mind*. Oxford: Oxford University Press, pp. 267–288 (1992).

Farrell, Warren, *The Myth of Male Power: Why Men Are the Disposable Sex*, New York: Simon & Schuster (1993).

Filer, Randall K., 'Male-female wage differences: The importance of compensating differentials', *Industrial and Labor Relations Review*, 38, 426–437 (1985).

Fuchs, Victor, *Women's Quest for Economic Equality*, Cambridge, MA: Harvard University Press (1988).

Goldin, Claudia, *Understanding the Gender Gap: An Economic History of American Workers*, New York: Oxford University Press (1990).

Roback, Jennifer, 'Beyond equality', *Georgetown Law Journal*, 82(1), 121–133 (1993).

Schwartz, Felice N., *Breaking with Tradition: Women and Work, The New Facts of Life*, New York: Warner Books (1992).

CHAPTER 6: Feminism and the Status of Women in the Workplace

Frankenhaeuser, Marianne, 'Challenge-control interaction as reflected in sympathetic-adrenal and pituitary-adrenal activity: Comparison between the sexes. *Scandinavian Journal of Psychology*, Supp. I, 158–164 (1982).

Mahony, Rhona, *Kidding Ourselves: Breadwinning, Babies, and Bargaining Power*, New York: BasicBooks (1995).

Okin, Susan M., *Justice, Gender, and the Family*, New York: Basic Books (1989).

Sommers, Christina Hoff, *Who Stole Feminism? How Women Have Betrayed Women*, New York: Simon & Schuster (1994).

CONCLUSION

Chomsky, Noam, *Reflections on Language*, New York: Pantheon (1975).

Levin, Michael, *Feminism and Freedom*, New Brunswick, NJ: Transaction (1987).